FREUD'S DA VINCI

D0927469

Mark Podwal, M.D.

IMAGES GRAPHIQUES, INC.
New York

AN IMAGES GRAPHIQUES BOOK
© Copyright 1977 Images Graphiques, Inc.
All rights reserved, which includes the right to reprint
this book or portions thereof in any form whatsoever.

IMAGES GRAPHIQUES INC.
37 Riverside Drive
New York, New York 10023

Library of Congress Catalog Card Number: 77-82799

ISBN Softcover Edition 0-89545-003-8
ISBN Hardcover Edition 0-89545-002-X

First Printing, July 1977

Printed in the United States of America

For my Uncle Julie

". . . biographers are fixated
on their heroes in quite
a special way . . . ."

Sigmund Freud

INTRODUCTION

"Perhaps the most famous left-handed individual was Leonardo [da Vinci], who is not known to have had any love-affairs."

Thus wrote Sigmund Freud to Fliess in 1898. That astounding recognition opened a door for Freud and threw a brilliant light on what for a duller man would have been nothing more than possible and feeble implications concerning:

Art,

Left-handedness, and

Sex.

But Freud—not a dull man—plunged ahead, perhaps blinded by that brilliant light, after verification of the implications.

In 1907, in response to a question concerning his favorite books, Freud mentions Merezhkovsky's **The Romance of Leonardo da Vinci.**

In a 1909 letter to Carl Jung, Freud discusses one of his patients who possessed Leonardo's "disposition" but "lacked" his genius.

The plunge after verification continued, as headlong as the best of them, and as surely destined to end in world-wide scandal, as is the wont of most.

By 1910, Freud's identification with da Vinci, though not explicitly articulated, is obvious. Of Leonardo, he quoted Merezhkovsky:

"He was like a man who awoke too early in the darkness while the others were all still asleep." Enlightened by Ernest Jones, can we not safely say that Freud was speaking as much of himself as of da Vinci in citing the quote?

Freud's study of da Vinci did cause a world-wide scandal when it was first published in 1910. And, for whatever complex of reasons, the study was to be Freud's only attempt at "psycho-biography."

But what had Freud done, really? He had drawn on and examined the peculiarities of da Vinci's personality—such as his obsession with flight, his sexual abstinence, his inability to complete his greatest works—and from this examination he had drawn a fascinating portrait of a man already acknowledged as the greatest of the Renaissance artists. Advertently or inadvertently, consciously or unconsciously, deliberately or not, Freud had also given us a portrait of himself, the analyst.

But art historians and literary critics were not concerned, let alone charmed, with the latter portrait. Rather, they rose nearly as a body, and bitterly accused (eschewing for the nonce the gray tones usually cloaking their pronouncements) Freud of Gross Errors and Glaring Omissions in his attempts to support his theories.

How, they cried out, dare Freud defame the genius of the Renaissance by asserting that Leonardo's prophetic flying machines were based on Sublimated Sexual Desire!

How, they asked, more in anger than bewilderment, could Freud say that Leonardo's marvelously detailed anatomical drawings stemmed from the artist's own Inability to Love?

Where they might have whimpered in pain, they thundered in rage: How, in all seriousness (When to be sane is to be serious), could Freud say that Leonardo's painting of "The Virgin and St. Anne" was really a portrait of the da Vinci family, with Leonardo himself as the Christ Child?

Freud was astute enough to anticipate the public attack. In the book's preface, Freud defends his approach. [Ed. note: Perhaps this was Freud's one Grave Error, in that it is universally accepted that no one reads the Preface to a book.] Psychiatric research, he states:

> ". . . cannot help finding worthy of understanding everything that can be recognized in these historical figures, and it

believes there is no one so great as to be disgraced by being subject to the laws which govern both normal and pathological activity with equal cogency."

But Freud should have known, or been told, that even if it is read, it takes more than an astucious preface to blunt the attack of a public mobilized by shock. Although Freud's study has managed to find admirers and supporters, it has been consistently rejected with explicit horror by the vast majority of Leonardo scholars, preface or no preface.

To wit: Leonardo's obsession with birds and flight (**see** Plate 3, 5). Freud interprets this in several ways. But he draws heavily on, and interprets extensively the "childhood memory" of Leonardo. In Leonardo's own words:

> "It seems that I was always destined to be so deeply concerned with vultures; for I recall as one of my very earliest memories that while I was in the cradle, a vulture came down to me, opened my mouth with its tail, and struck me many times with its tail against my lips."

This "memory" was not really a memory at all, said Freud, but a fantasy which Leonardo formed later in life and which, for various reasons, he chose to locate in the time of his childhood. Further, Freud postulates, Leonardo had discovered, among his father's books, the Greek belief that vultures were an all-female species. Reproduction occurred, presumably, when a vulture stopped in mid-flight, opened its vagina, and was fertilized by the wind. Freud believed that this notion of reproduction without impregnation by a male may possibly have formed the basis of Leonardo's vulture fantasy. He theorized that Leonardo had already identified himself as a "vulture-child," or one who had a mother, but lacked a father.

What is obviously the most serious criticism of Freud's thesis is that the bird which visited Leonardo in his "childhood memory" was a **kite,** not a vulture. Freud's error can be traced to an erroneous translation in the text he read.

Staunch supporters of Freud have argued that a kite is, nevertheless and after all, a bird. As a counter-measure or challenge, this was as effective a defensive strategem as daisies strewn in the path of Ghengis Khan.

Freud's lengthy discussion of vulture mythology and the Egyptian deity Mut (**see** Plate 6) were **irrelevant.** Freud was, nonetheless, obstinately reluctant to renounce his vulture theory.

Setting aside the matter of the mistranslation—it would be of interest only to the translator's analyst or editor—let us look more closely, as others have, at Freud's refusal to renounce his own error.

If the "vulture-mother" was not, in fact, da Vinci's, then it appears not at all unreasonable to conjecture that it was Freud's. Among the more interesting dreams discussed in **The Interpretation of Dreams** (1900), is the one from Freud's own childhood, of the bird-headed gods. Analysts have proposed that it was this bird dream which further strengthened Freud's identification with Leonardo.

The noted art historian Meyer Schapiro offers evidence that Freud knowingly and willingly distorted facts concerning Leonardo's earliest years in order to suit his theories.

It has also been suggested that Freud owed his "two mother" interpretation of "The Virgin and St. Anne" (**see** Plate 2) to the two mothers of his own childhood: his real mother and his Catholic nanny.

Further from the mark, though there among the outraged, are the critics who point out that Freud in his analysis made no attempt to account for Leonardo's genius. However, on numerous occasions, Freud responded that "where the artist gets his ability to create is no concern of psychology." He maintained that psychoanalysis does not attempt to explain genius, but endeavors to study the laws governing man's mind as exemplified in outstanding personages.

But, to attend only to all of this furor over Freud's unsupported analysis of Leonardo is to have missed the central, perhaps the pivotal point: Freud may have been right about Leonardo in every instance, and there may be yet undiscovered a sketchbook which may show that Freud was cautious, even conservative in his analysis.

The writings found in the numerous extant manuscripts and notebooks of Leonardo are described by Freud as being chaste or "one might say even abstinent. . . . It is well known how frequently great artists take pleasure in giving vent to their fantasies in erotic and even crudely obscene pictures. In Leonardo's case, on the contrary, we have only some anatomical sketches of the internal female genitals, the position of the embryo in the womb, and so on."

Freud's study of **The Moses of Michaelangelo** (1914) was accompanied by theoretical sketches to illustrate the thesis. So why not theoretical sketches for Freud's study of Leonardo, while we wait for the discovery of the inexplicably lost sketchbook?

These then, are the drawings Freud would like to have discovered among Leonardo's "abstinent" manuscripts. And with the publication of this volume, Freud's wish may have been fulfilled.

One wants somehow to help Freud solve the enigma of the Mona Lisa's smile, when Freud was the one who had selected a line from **Oedipus the King** for his epitaph: "He was a man most mighty who solved the riddle of the Sphinx."

—Mark Podwal, M.D.
    New York City
    June, 1977

THE PLATES

THE PLATES

PLATE 1

STUDY FOR
"THE VIRGIN OF THE ROCKS"

The celebrated "Oedipus Complex" refers to the love a male child feels for his mother, coupled with his fear of being castrated by his supposed rival—his father—should the love be discovered. To conceal the love and thereby avoid castration, the child identifies with the father. A child who lacks a father "image"—through actual or emotional separation—or who has a weak father and a domineering mother, will instead identify with the mother. A possible homosexual pattern is thus initiated.

Leonardo was the illegitimate son of Ser Piero, a notary, who married one Donna Albiera the year Leonardo was born. The first few years of Leonardo's life were spent with his real mother, Caterina, a peasant girl. Ser Piero later allowed Leonardo to live with him when Donna Albiera could not bear him a child.

PLATE 2

MARY-ANNE COLLAGE

Over the years, art critics have commented on
the fact that in "The Virgin and St. Anne," Mary's
mother is portrayed as young and radiant as her
daughter. Furthermore, in a preliminary study for
the painting the two figures are so fused that it
appears "as if two heads were growing from a
single body." To Freud, this composition
represents Leonardo's memories of the two
mothers of his own childhood: Caterina, his real
mother, and Donna Albiera, his stepmother.

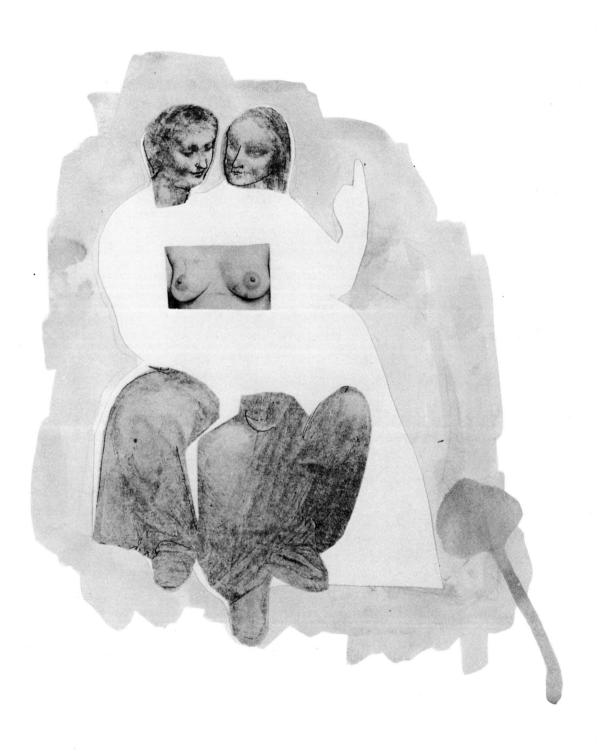

PLATE 3

VULTURE CUT OUT AS TWO BREASTS

Freud interprets Leonardo's obsession
with birds and flight in several ways.

PLATE 4

VIBRATING TONGUE

If we examine Leonardo's vulture fantasy through
Freud's eyes, we discover its highly erotic content:
A tail is among the more common symbols for
the male genitalia. The fantasy of a vulture's tail
striking about inside the child's mouth
symbolically represents the act of fellatio.

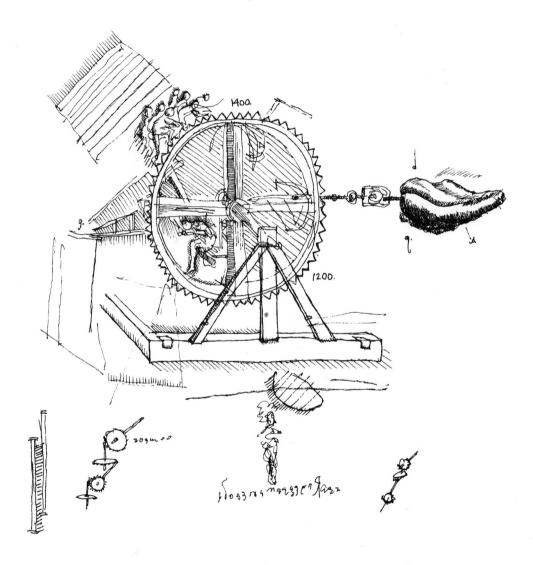

PLATE 5

VULTURE CUT OUT,
AS THE MOTHER OF GOD AND HER CHILD

"What the fantasy conceals is merely a reminiscence of sucking—or being suckled—at his mother's breast, a scene of human beauty that he, like so many artists, undertook to depict with his brush, in the guise of the mother of God and her child," notes Freud.

PLATE 6

THE GODDESS MUT IN THE SIXTH AND THE NINTH MONTHS OF GESTATION

Freud offers an explanation as to how Leonardo was able to unconsciously transform the mother figure of the vulture into a symbol for the male genitalia: In ancient Egyptian hieroglyphics, explains Freud, "mother" is represented by a picture of a vulture. The Egyptians worshipped a mother goddess (decidedly female) whose name was pronounced "MUT." This goddess was depicted with the head of a vulture, breasts of a woman, and phallus of a man.

Freud admits that the possibility of this information filtering down to Leonardo is extremely remote. But he offers it nonetheless.

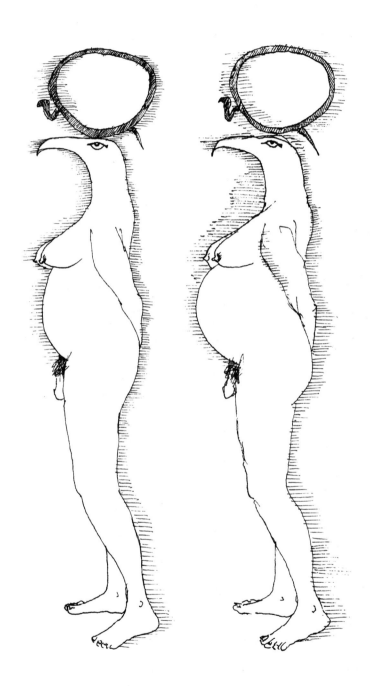

PLATE 7

STUDY FOR A FOUNTAIN

According to psychoanalytic theories of infantile
sexual behavior, there is a period of
development when the male child finds it
inconceivable that the penis, such an essential
member of his body, is absent in others. First, he
concludes that little girls also have a penis, but a
tiny one, that will later grow to full size.

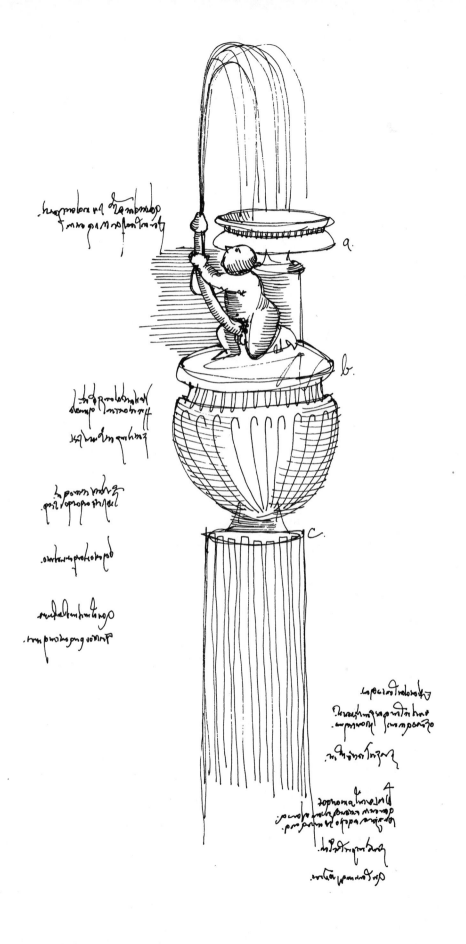

PLATE 8

DETAILS OF SCYTHED CAR

A male child, realizing that little girls lack even a
tiny penis, assumes that it has been cut off and
that what remains is the wound. He now fears
even more for his own masculinity.

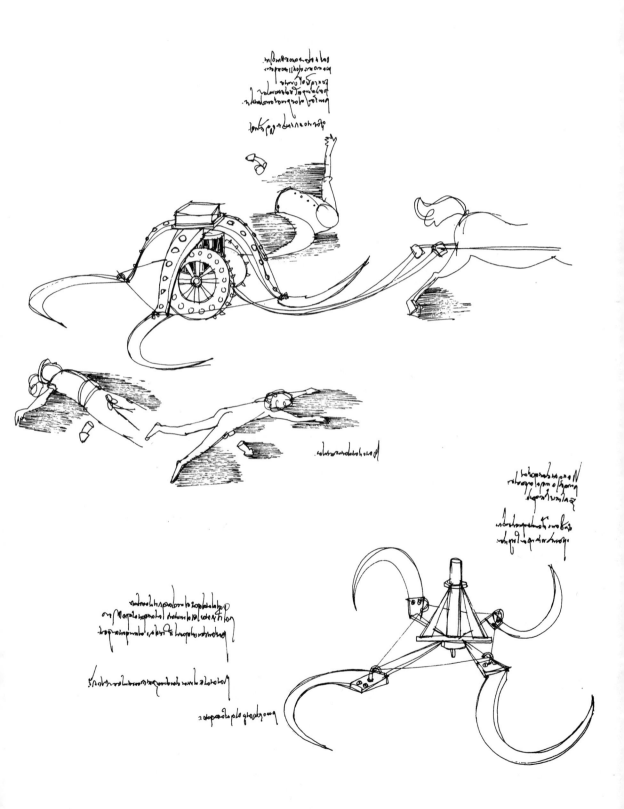

PLATE 9

MAP OF ITALY, FETISH CUT OUT

Psychoanalytic tradition holds that fetishism is based upon the patient (usually male) not acknowledging the fact that females lack a penis. The truth is extremely distasteful to the patient since it reinforces his own castration anxieties. The patient denies what his senses perceive and a substitute object (usually a body part) assumes the role of the missing penis. Common fetishes include a woman's foot and shoe. The substituted object is often something the patient noted at the very moment he first viewed the female genitalia.

PLATE 10

DEVICE FOR INDUCING
AND MAINTAINING AN ERECTION

In certain individuals, the final realization that
women lack a penis is associated with a repulsion
towards females. Sometimes this may cause
psychological impotence.

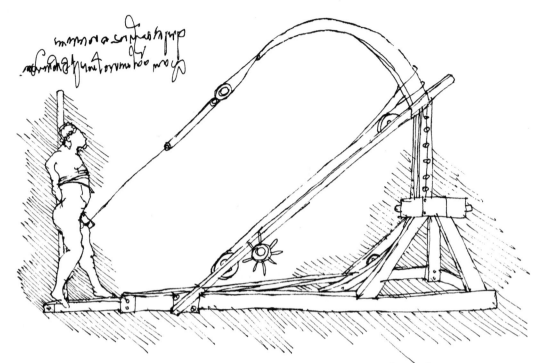

PLATE 11

FLIGHT FANTASY
BASED ON A SKETCH BY LEONARDO

The bird in Leonardo's childhood memory,
coupled with the artist's later obsession with flight,
has further significance for Freud: Those who are
preoccupied with flight long for sexual
satisfaction.

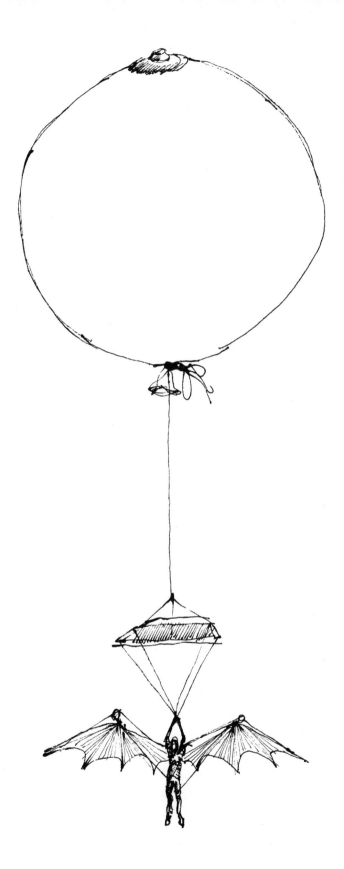

PLATE 12

STUDY OF BIRD
OUTSTRETCHING ITS WING

There are numerous examples in language of
the association of sexual activity with the flight of
birds. The German expression for male sexual
activity is "vögeln" ("to bird"). In Italian, the male
organ is called "L'uccello" ("the bird").

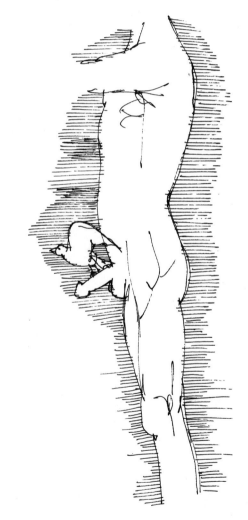

PLATE 13

STUDY FOR
"LEDA AND THE SWAN"

Curious children who ask where babies come from are often told that they are delivered by the stork. To Freudians, the stork is merely the representation of a winged phallus.

PLATE 14

AN AURAL FIXATION

Psychoanalytic investigation teaches us that at
about the age of three, the infant becomes
curious as to where babies come from. This
interest is often first aroused by the birth of a
sibling. Explanations offered by parents involving
the stork are surprisingly rejected by the inquisitive
infant. Freud states that the infant's ''intellectual
independence'' begins with this ''act of disbelief''
and that the child never quite forgives his parents
for trying to deceive him about the facts of life.
The infant then goes on to develop his own
theories.

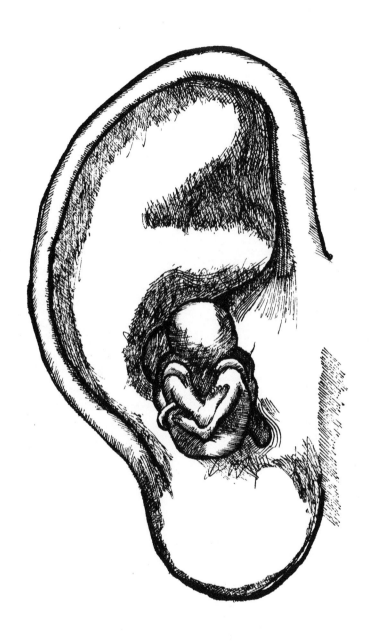

PLATE 15

LEONARDO'S AERIAL SCREW

The helicopter, or "aerial screw" (Leonardo's own words) was to ascend by the same aerodynamic principle as the modern propeller-driven airplane.

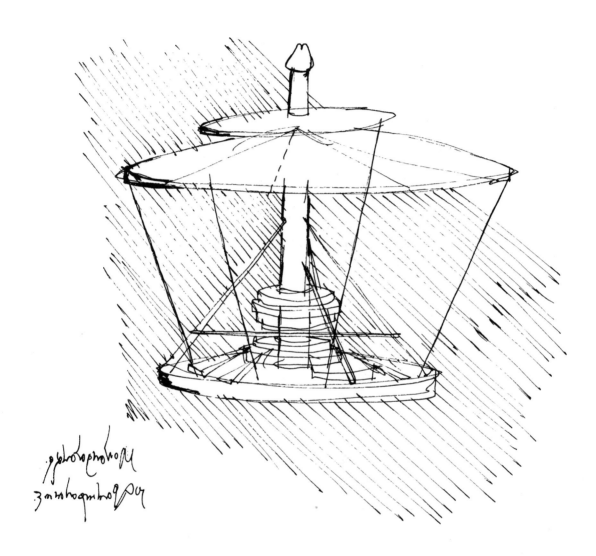

PLATE 16

UNFINISHED STUDY FOR
"THE CANON OF PROPORTIONS"

If each creative artist feels like a father towards his own work, then Leonardo's relationship with his own father proved destructive. Freud notes: "He created them (his paintings) and then cared no more about them, just as his father had not cared about him."

Confronted with the fact that Ser Piero did care about his son—if belatedly—Freud counters that it was too late: Impressions incurred in early infancy cannot be rectified by later happenings.

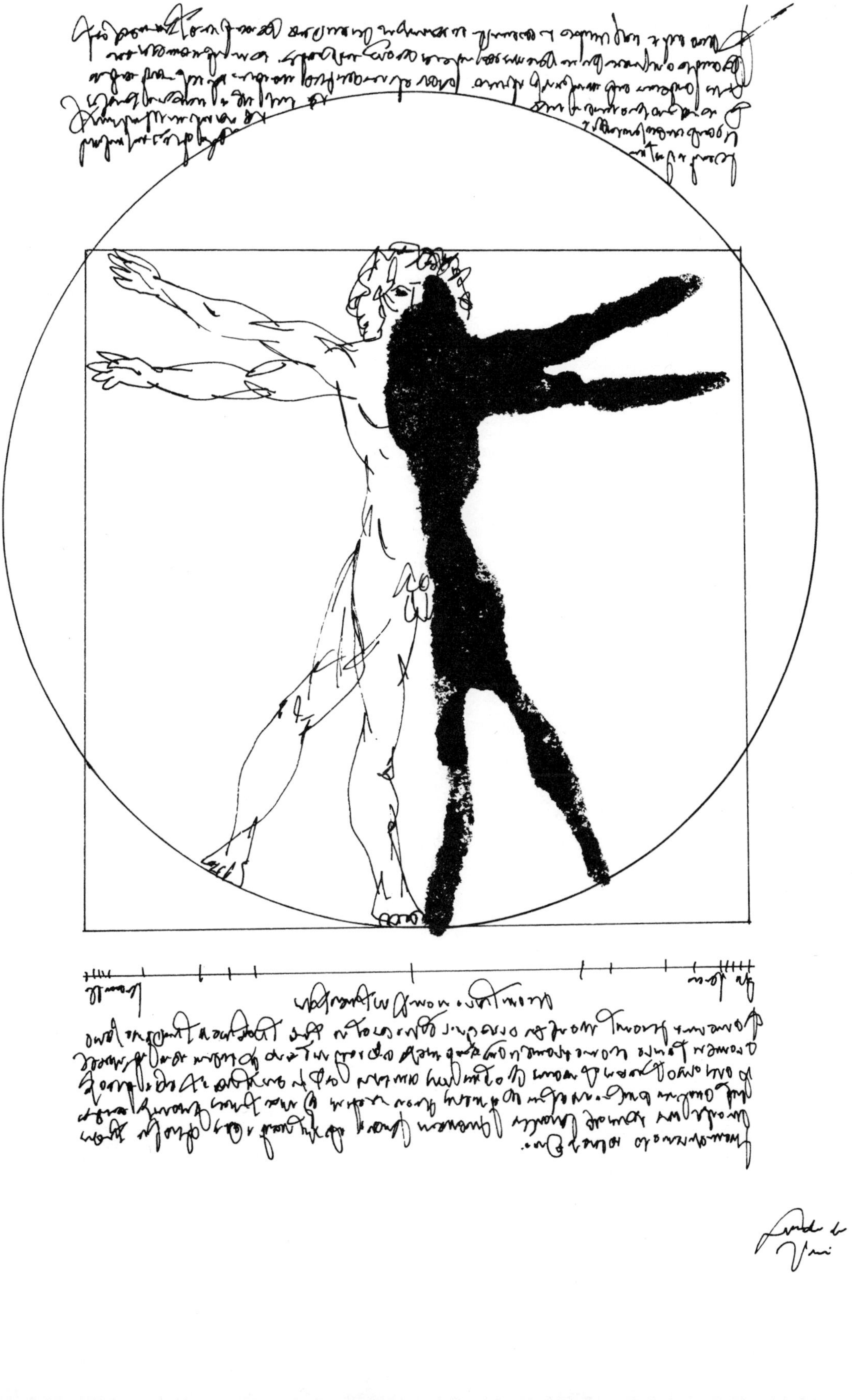

PLATE 17

STUDY FOR THE PORTRAIT
OF COUNTESS ISABELLA D'ESTE

In sublimation, energies normally directed
towards sexual gratification are discharged in
other endeavors. Freud notes that **complete**
suppression of sexual activity does not provide
"the most favorable conditions" for sublimation.

In his later years, Leonardo turned toward
scientific experimentation and away from
painting. Countess Isabella d'Este, who desired to
possess one of Leonardo's paintings no matter
the cost, remarked sadly that the artist had
become "most impatient with the brush."

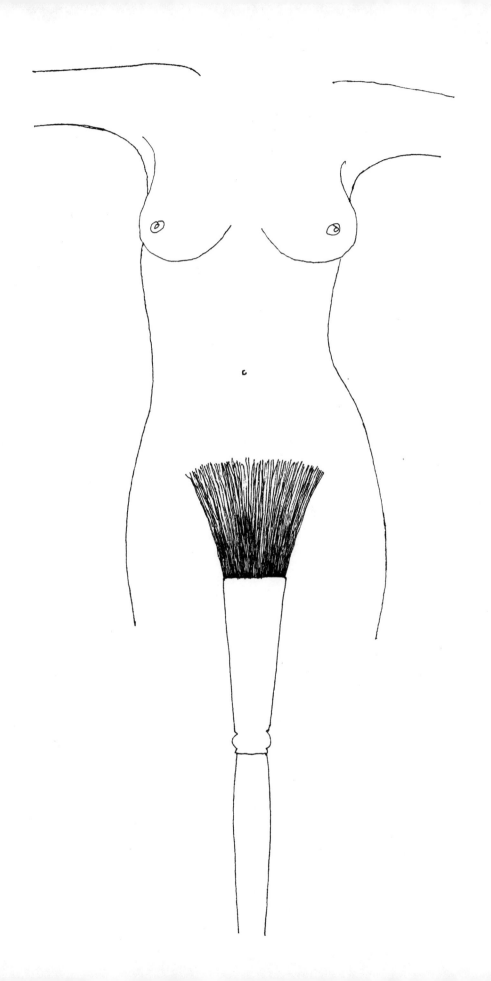

PLATE 18

CANNON FOUNDRY

Guns and cannons are, according to
psychoanalytic theory, symbolic extensions
of the male sexual organ.

PLATE 19

MIRROR WRITING AND PLANT STUDIES:
COIX LACHRYMA L. AND SPARGANIUM ERECTUM L.

A common belief is that Leonardo wrote backwards (so-called "mirror writing") in order to conceal his thoughts, since he was afraid of ecclesiastical persecution. However, many art historians feel Leonardo wrote backwards simply because he was left-handed.

PLATE 20

ARTIFICIAL INSEMINATION DEVICE

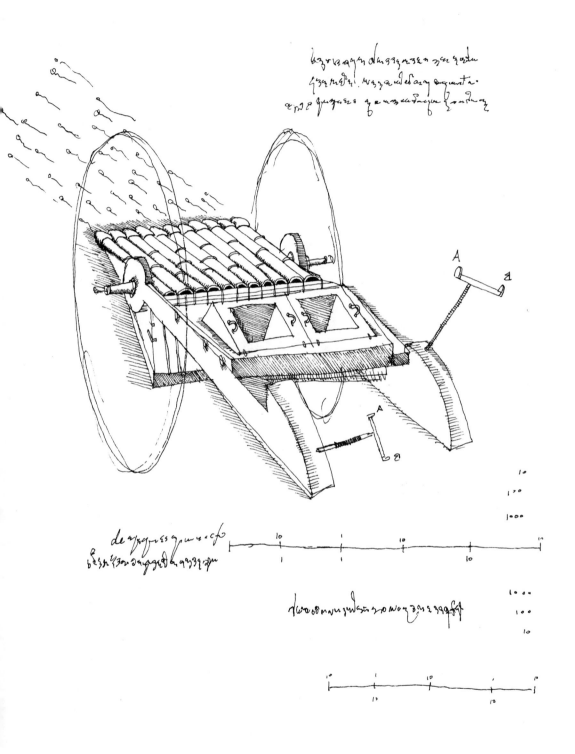

PLATE 21

ARTIFICIAL INSEMINATION DEVICE
NO. 2

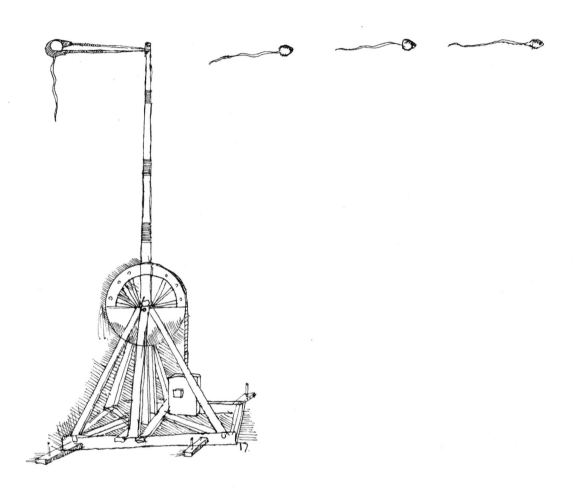

PLATE 22

COMPASS AND PUBIC TRIANGLE

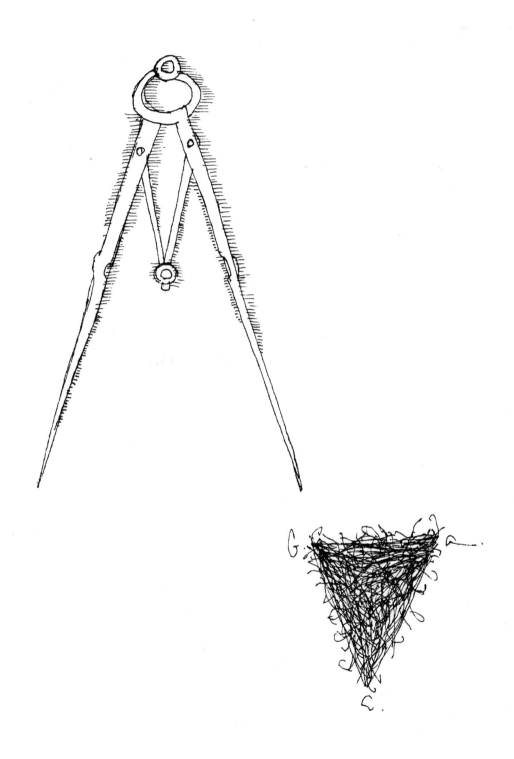

PLATE 23

VAGINA WITH TEETH

Horror Feminae (fear of women) is experienced by many overt homosexuals when suddenly confronted by a sexually aroused woman.

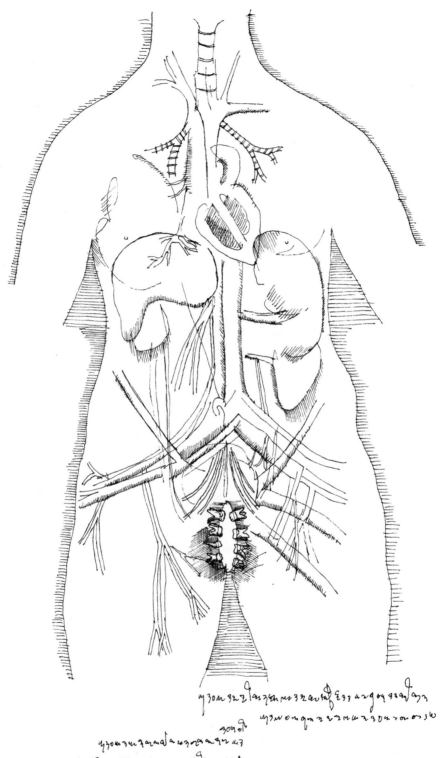

PLATE 24

PUBIC CRABS AND
THEIR PLACE OF HABITATION

Freudian theory holds that the persistent
anxiety of castration may take the form of
syphilophobia (the fear of acquiring a
serious disease through sexual relations).

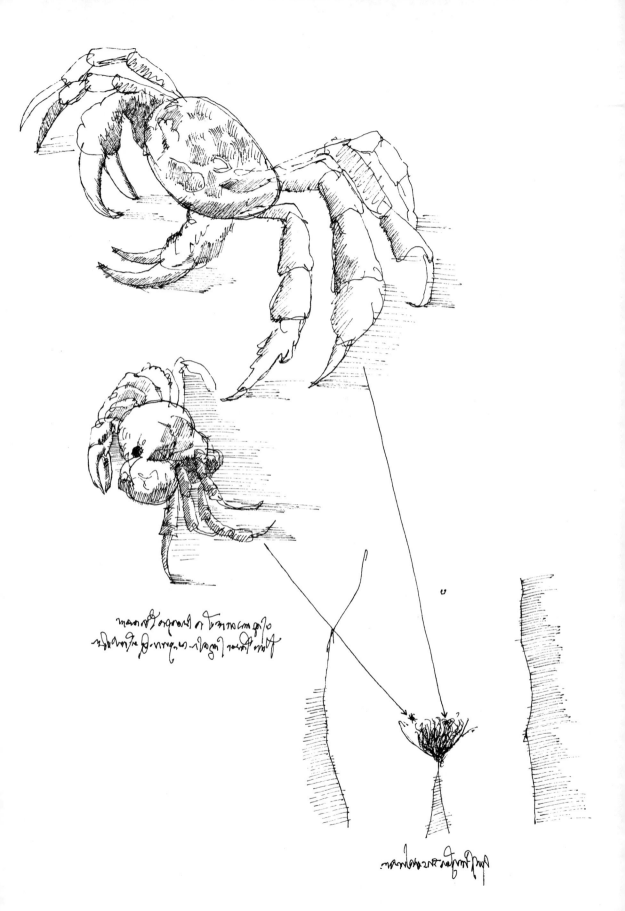

PLATE 25

FORTIFICATION TO PREVENT
THE SPREAD OF VENEREAL DISEASE

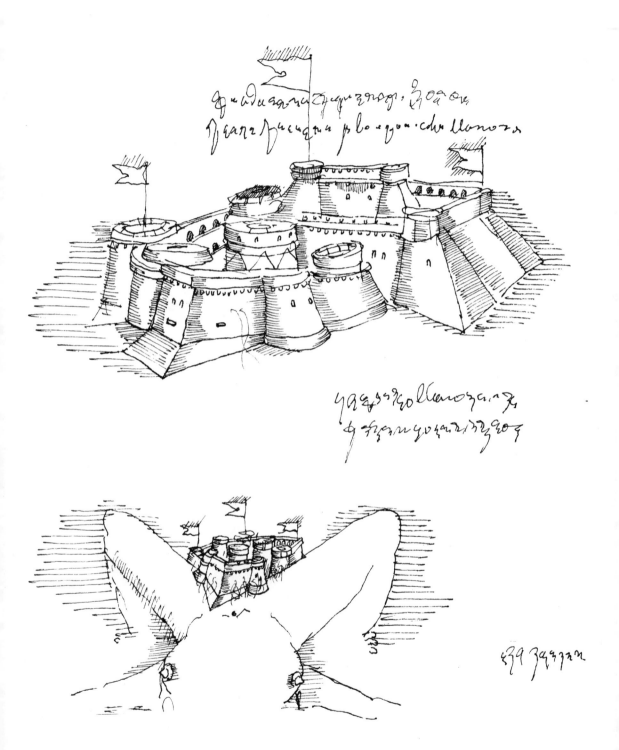

PLATE 26

MACHINE WITH FEATHERS
(FOR TICKLING)

PLATE 27

HUGGING MACHINE

E. Solmi, in his work, **Leonardo da Vinci,**
attributes the following quotation to Leonardo:

"The act of procreation and everything
that has any relation to it is so disgusting
that human beings would soon die out
if it were not a traditional custom, and if
there were no pretty faces and
sensuous dispositions."

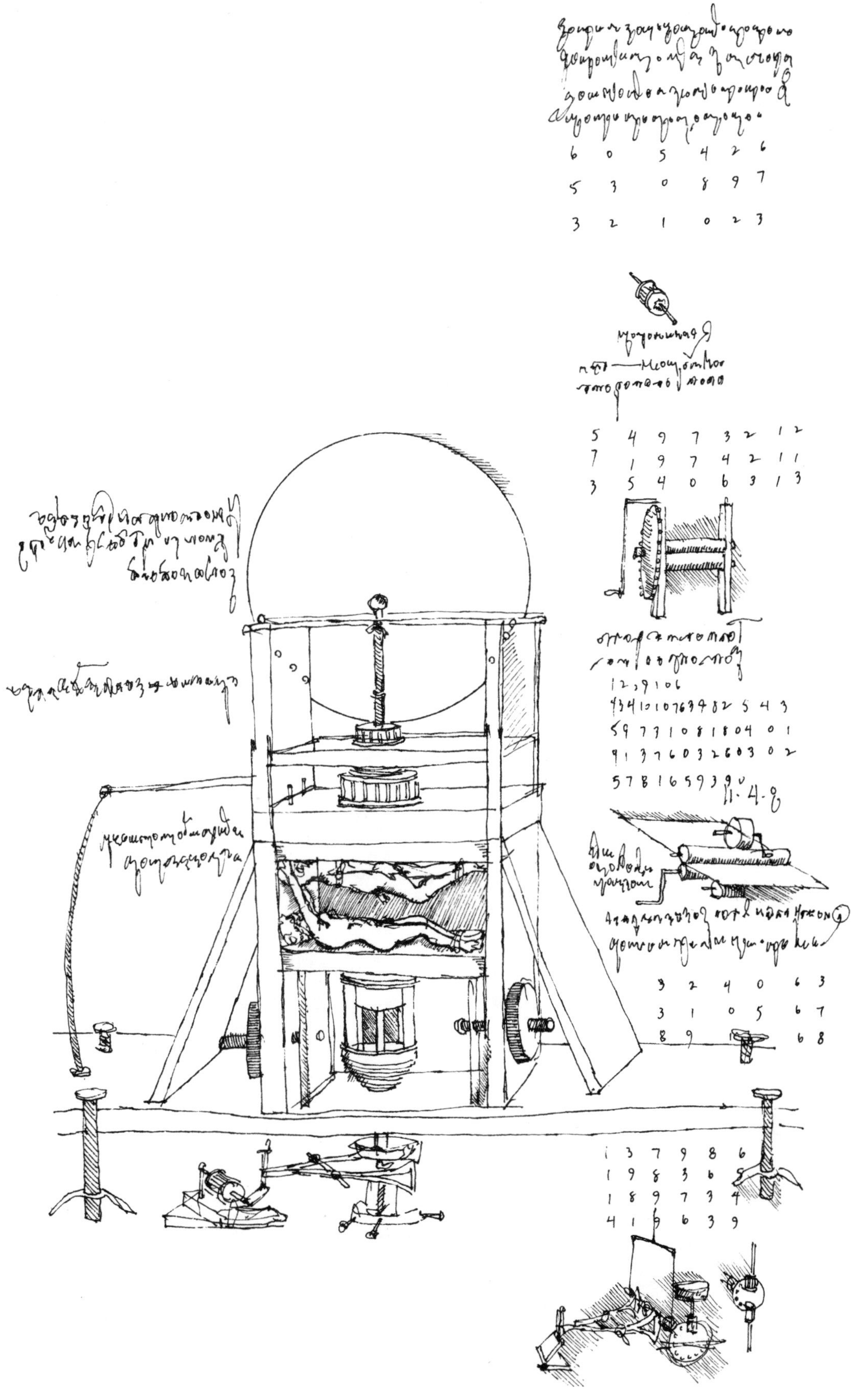

PLATE 28

SCREWING DEVICE

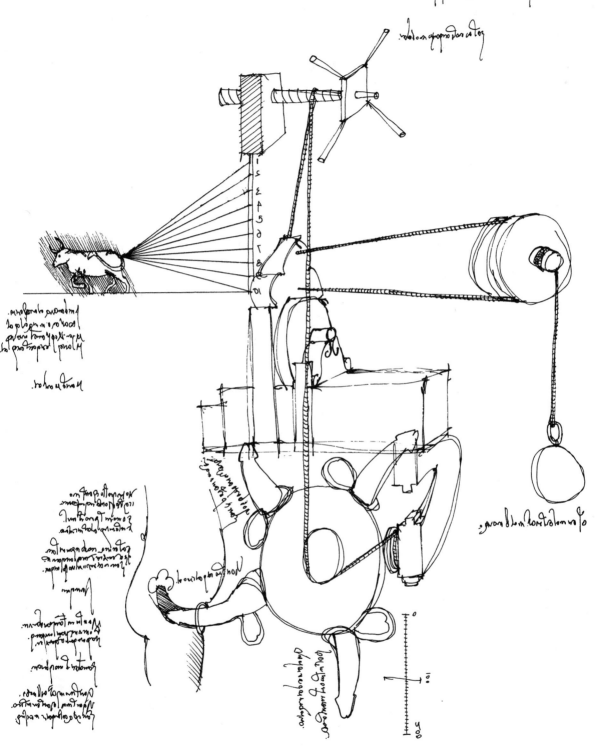

PLATE 29

MEMORIAL TO THE DUKE OF SFORZA
FOR THE USE OF HIS WIDOW

According to Freud, a common neurosis in
women is the repressed wish to possess a penis.
This infantile desire is termed "penis-envy."

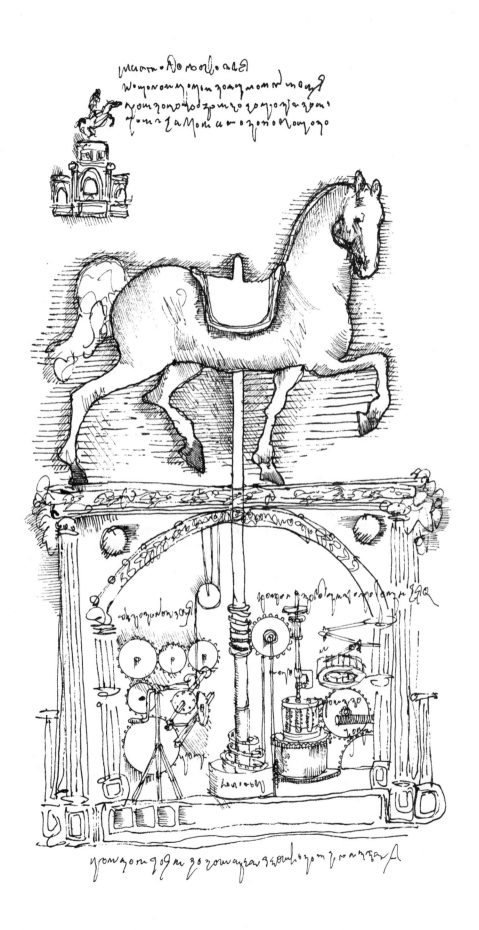

PLATE 30

CHURCH OF OUR HOLY MOTHER

Psychoanalysis describes the "intimate
connection" between the "father complex" and
a belief in God ("an exalted Father-figure").
Leonardo, deprived of a father during the
earliest years of childhood, was, according to
Freud, unlikely to remain a follower of "dogmatic
religion." During his lifetime, Leonardo was, in
fact, often accused of straying from the Church's
teachings.

PLATE 31

AUTOPSY STUDY OF BARONCELLI, ASSASSIN OF GIULIANO DE MEDICI

The Church was fully aware of Leonardo's scientific researches and the cadavers he studied were dissected in ecclesiastical hospitals, such as Santa Maria Nuovo in Florence. The Pope was more concerned with the speed of Leonardo's efforts than with his religious views.

PLATE 32

CARS FOR ASSAULTING FORTRESSES

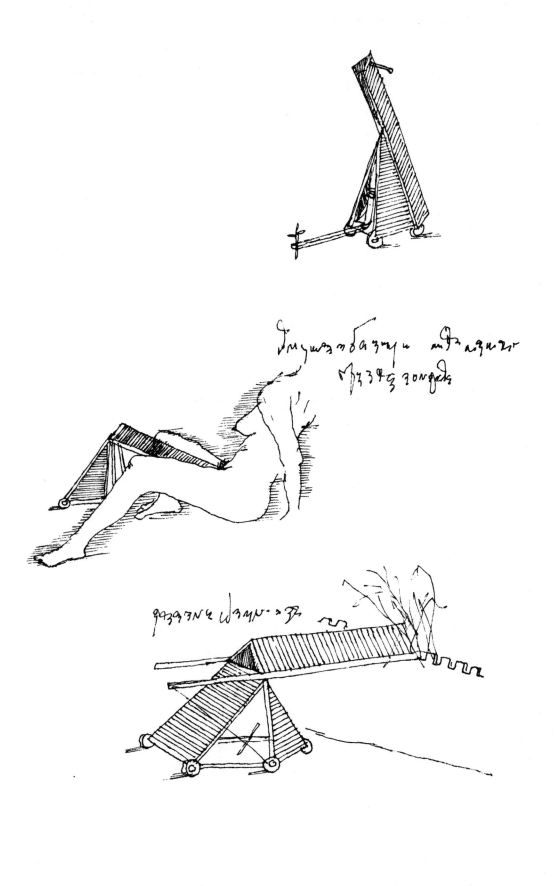

PLATE 33

**DEFENSE OF BASTION
BY MEANS OF BOMBARD FIRE**

PLATE 34

UNFINISHED STUDY
FOR THE BATTLE OF ANGHIARI

The Battle of Anghiari, which Leonardo began
painting on a wall of the Sala del Consiglio in
Florence, was similary doomed because of his
endless technical experimentation. Leonardo
finally abandoned the painting—incomplete.

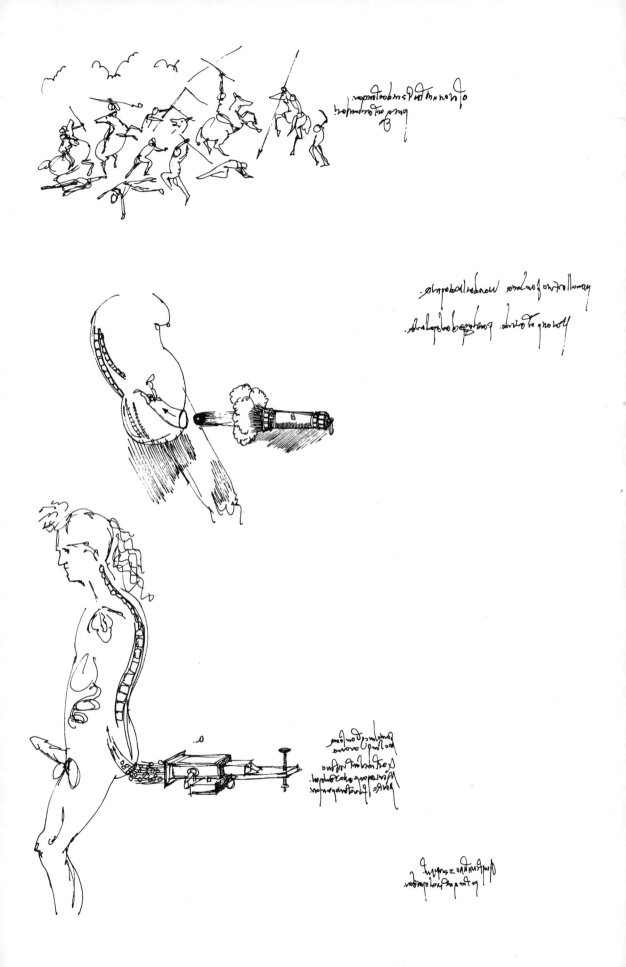

PLATE 35

ALLEGORICAL COMPOSITION

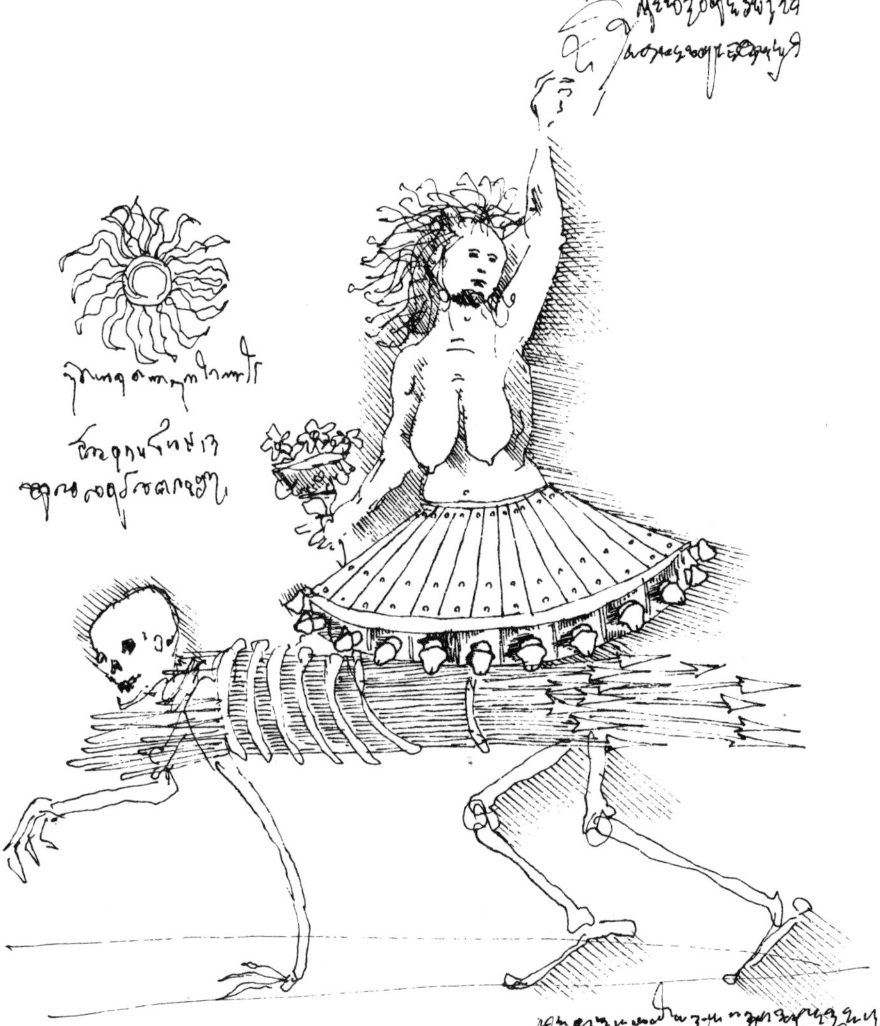

PLATE 36

BUST OF A WARRIOR

Freud was by no means the first
to point out that many of the males
in Leonardo's paintings possess
effeminate characteristics.

PLATE 37

ONE MAN BAND

At sixteen, while serving as an apprentice to the artist Verrocchio, Leonardo, along with some other young men, was charged with homosexual activities. Leonardo "fell under suspicion because he had employed a boy of poor reputation as one of his models." He was ultimately acquitted, and even Freud concedes Leonardo was probably innocent of the charges.

In later years, Leonardo surrounded himself with handsome young pupils, few of whom possessed "significant talent." His associations with the many young men who shared his life did not, according to Freud, extend to sexual activity. Significantly, Freud never charges Leonardo with overt homosexuality.

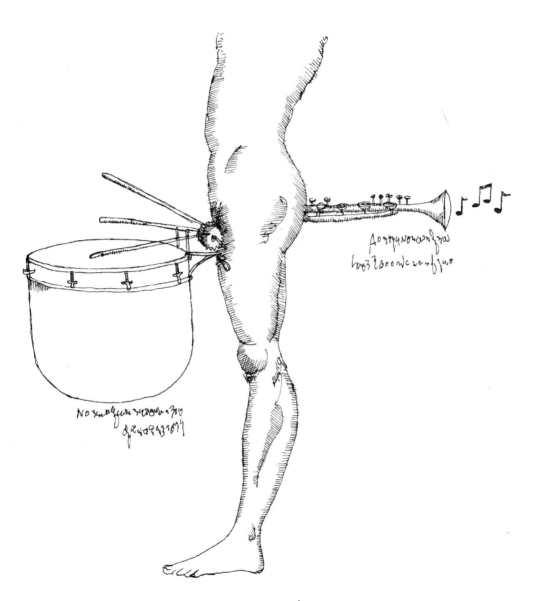

PLATE 38

STUDY FOR
THE PORTRAIT OF MONA LISA

Everyone is struck by the Mona Lisa's elusive
smile; a smile which, if one looks closely,
Leonardo later transferred to every face he
painted, including that of St. John the Baptist.

Freud suspects it was Caterina, Leonardo's
mother, who first possessed that evocative,
almost taunting, smile—a smile which Leonardo
remembered from his infancy. Leonardo
rediscovered it on Mona Lisa del Giocondo and
painted it again and again.

Leonardo never considered the Mona Lisa quite
finished, and never delivered it to the person for
whom it was painted.

L.H.O.O.Q.

PLATE 39

KISSING MACHINE

Leonardo's contemporaries were often
puzzled by the artist "wasting" his time
constructing elaborate toys for festivals.

PLATE 40

INFANTILE SELF-PORTRAIT

"Nevertheless, psychoanalysis still cannot explain
Leonardo's extraordinary capacity for sublimating
the primitive instincts."

—Sigmund Freud, 1910

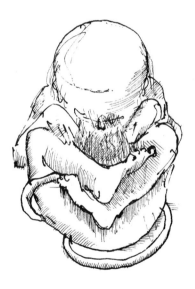

Acknowledgments

Readers are encouraged to read Freud's original study of
Leonardo, **Leonardo da Vinci—A Memory of His Childhood.** The
edition which I consulted and quoted from in this volume was
translated by Alan Tyson and published by W. W. Norton, New York.

The publication of this volume would not have been possible
without the help and encouragement of many individuals. First, I
would like to thank Dr. John Schwartz, who introduced me to my
publisher, Jack Rennert. Jack not only grasped the concept from
the onset, but personally saw it through its long gestation period.
Marion Fredi Towbin's help was essential in the writing of the text.
Jane Wagner's pen was also indispensable. Helen Garfinkle did
what she could. Harry Chester and his staff were responsible for
aesthetic considerations. Andy Merson followed through with
careful production.

And, finally, to my wife Ayalah, whose ideas and discussions
were of invaluable assistance.

—Mark Podwal, M. D.